P9-DBP-270

BLAIRSVILLE SENIOR HIGH SCHOOL
BLAIRSVILLE, PENNA.

Chad Johnson

Frank Angst
AR B.L.: 5.9 Alt.: 908
Points: 2.0   MG

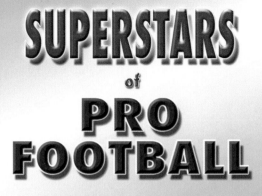

SUPERSTARS
of
PRO FOOTBALL

CHAD JOHNSON

Frank Angst

Mason Crest Publishers

Produced by OTTN Publishing in association with
21st Century Publishing and Communications, Inc.

MASON CREST PUBLISHERS INC.
370 Reed Road
Broomall, Pennsylvania 19008
(866) MCP-BOOK (toll free)
www.masoncrest.com

Printed in the United States of America.

First Printing

9 8 7 6 5 4 3 2 1

Library of Congress Cataloging-in-Publication Data

Angst, Frank.
   Chad Johnson / Frank Angst.
      p. cm. — (Superstars of pro football)
   Includes index.
   ISBN 978-1-4222-0556-3 (hardcover) — ISBN 978-1-4222-0826-7 (pbk.)
   1. Johnson, Chad, 1978–   —Juvenile literature. 2. Football players—United
States—Biography—Juvenile literature. 3. Cincinnati Bengals (Football team).
I. Title.
GV939.J6125A54 2008
796.33092—dc22
[B]   2008024185

Publisher's note:
All quotations in this book come from original sources, and contain the spelling
and grammatical inconsistencies of the original text.

◄◄ CROSS-CURRENTS ►►

In the ebb and flow of the currents of life we are each influenced
by many people, places, and events that we directly experience or
have learned about. Throughout the chapters of this book you will
come across **CROSS-CURRENTS** reference bubbles. These bubbles
direct you to a **CROSS-CURRENTS** section in the back of the
book that contains fascinating and informative sidebars
and related pictures. Go on. ►►

◄◄CONTENTS►►

1 Ocho Cinco's Promise 4

2 Long Road to Stardom 10

3 Earning His Stripes 16

4 Time to Celebrate 26

5 Future Hall of Famer? 36

Cross-Currents 46

Chronology 54

Accomplishments & Awards 55

Further Reading & Internet Resources 57

Glossary 58

Notes 60

Index 62

Picture Credits 64

About the Author 64

OCHO CINCO'S PROMISE

It was the final game of the Cincinnati Bengals' 2007 regular season. On his first catch of the game, Bengals receiver Chad Johnson pulled in a two-yard touchdown pass to score against the Miami Dolphins. On his second catch, Chad cut over the middle and hauled in a 15-yard pass from quarterback Carson Palmer. Then he unleashed his speed.

Chad slipped by Dolphins safety Jason Allen. Miami's other safety, Lance Schulters, gave chase, but Chad was too fast. In the blink of an eye, he raced into the end zone for a 70-yard touchdown.

Chad had scored two touchdowns in just two catches.

Chad Johnson (lower right) takes off at the start of a play against the Miami Dolphins, December 30, 2007. Chad caught four passes for 131 yards and two touchdowns as the Bengals defeated the Dolphins, 38-25.

Returning Home

Chad enjoyed playing well against the Dolphins. He grew up in a Miami neighborhood called Liberty City. Many of his friends attended the game. Chad promised those friends something to see.

As usual, he kept his promise. Chad finished the game with four catches for 131 yards. He broke his own Bengals record for receiving yards in a season, with 1,440 yards. In 2007, Chad had five games with at least 100 receiving yards, tying his own team record.

Chad was disappointed the Bengals did not make the **playoffs**, but he was glad to help Cincinnati win the Miami game, 38-25. The Bengals would finish 2007 with a 7-9 win-loss record. That victory gave the Bengals back-to-back wins for the first time all season, however—and optimism for next year.

A few weeks later, Chad was selected to replace an injured Randy Moss in the Pro Bowl, the NFL's all-star game. It was the fifth straight time Johnson had been selected for this game. He was happy to join his Bengal teammate T.J. Houshmandzadeh, who made the Pro Bowl for the first time.

Top Performer

Many fans know Chad for his touchdown celebrations and his victory guarantees. Some also know Chad for his unusual nickname, "Ocho Cinco." In Spanish, "Ocho Cinco" means "Eight Five," Chad's number.

Chad has always matched his outgoing football personality with top play. In just seven NFL seasons, he has established himself as one of the best receivers in the NFL. He led the **American Football Conference** (AFC) in receiving yards for four years in a row, from 2003 to 2006. He is the first player ever to lead a conference in receiving for four straight years.

CROSS-CURRENTS

To learn more about the place where Chad's team plays its home games, read "Paul Brown Stadium." Go to page 46.

After scoring the first touchdown of the game—and of the Bengals' season—in a 2007 *Monday Night Football* game against the Baltimore Ravens, Chad put on a jacket that read, "Future H.O.F. 20??" "H.O.F." stands for Hall of Fame. The question marks represent not *whether* Chad will be voted in, but the year—as yet unknown—that Chad thinks himself likely to be inducted. Many NFL experts agree that Chad could make the Hall of Fame after he retires.

In the 2003 season, Chad was fined a total of $70,000 by the NFL. He was fined for uniform violations, including wearing orange shoes, and he was even fined $10,000 for holding up a sign that read, "Dear NFL, Please Don't Fine Me AGAIN!!!!," after scoring a touchdown in a win over the San Francisco 49ers.

Having Fun Playing Well

Chad's friend Steve Smith, also a Pro Bowl receiver, played with Chad in college. Smith told a *Sports Illustrated* reporter that Chad loves to have fun, but Chad does not let that fun stop him from playing his best:

Miami defender Jason Allen watches from the ground as Chad sprints toward the end zone. Chad's second touchdown against the Dolphins in the December 30 game was his eighth score of the 2007 season.

"He likes to be outspoken, to be out there a little bit. He loves the game so much, and he shows it. But he's not gonna go too far. Chad has been through too much to throw it all away."

Chad explained that he isn't trying to make the other team feel bad with his celebrations:

"How much of it is entertainment? All of it. I entertain. That's what I do. . . . I'm never going to be boring in the end zone. Fans don't want to see that. People paying $3,000 a **season ticket** don't want to see me hand the ball to the official. They want to see my personality."

Chad (number 85) is in the center of the second row in this Cincinnati Bengals team portrait from 2007. Since joining the Bengals in 2001, Chad has worked hard to turn the team into a consistent winner.

Helping the Bengals

Chad has played his entire NFL career with the Cincinnati Bengals. Before Chad joined the Bengals in 2001, the team had struggled to win games. The Bengals had reached the Super Bowl twice during the 1980s, and made the playoffs in 1990 with a 9-7 record. However, during the 1990s no team lost more games than Cincinnati. During the decade, the Bengals won 52 games and lost 108. The team's record did not get better in 2000 and 2001. The Bengals won a total of nine games in those two seasons.

After Chad was drafted, he promised to do his best to make Cincinnati a consistent winner. He told the media:

> **"I just want to tell the Bengals' organization that I won't let you down. I'm going to make Cincinnati my city. I'm going to give these people something they haven't had for years."**

Many fans doubted Chad could succeed in Cincinnati, but he has been true to his promise. Since he emerged as one of the NFL's top receivers in 2003, the Bengals have won more games than they have lost.

People who doubted Chad did not realize that he had been through many difficult times. He grew up in a tough neighborhood. He was kicked out of one college for fighting, and struggled to achieve good grades. In his only year of major college football, Chad nearly quit the team. Each time, however, Chad came back.

CROSS-CURRENTS

To learn more about the uniforms worn by Chad and his teammates, check out "Orange-and-Black Attack." Go to page 47.

LONG ROAD TO STARDOM

One day when Chad was young, he decided to ride a bike. He had just one problem: he had never sat on a bike before. Chad didn't have training wheels or adult help, but he hopped on anyway. His grandfather, James Flowers, saw Chad out the window and worried that he might get hurt. James yelled for Chad to stop.

Chad did not stop. He pedaled a few feet and then crashed to the pavement. Chad got back up, but he fell a second time. Now he had cuts and scrapes all over his legs. Still, Chad got back on the bike for a third time. A few minutes later, he raced past the window, pedaling at full speed.

Chad shows off his bike-riding skills during an ESPN event in Florida. As a child, Chad was always active and enjoyed playing sports. His grandmother remembered that Chad taught himself how to ride a bike without adult help.

Chad's grandmother, Bessie Mae Flowers, told *Sports Illustrated* about that day. She said that this story showed how Chad is willing to struggle for what he wants:

> **He will never admit he's hurt. He will be bleeding to death, and he will say, 'No, I'm O.K.'**

Growing Up in Miami

Born on January 9, 1978, Chad lived in Liberty City, a Miami neighborhood, with his mom Paula and his grandparents, Bessie and James Flowers. Chad never had much contact with his father.

A mural depicting Martin Luther King is shown on the side of a building in Liberty City. Liberty City is a Miami neighborhood where young Chad lived with his grandparents.

When Chad was five, his mother moved to Los Angeles for a job. She took Chad's younger brother Chauncey with her but left Chad to be raised by his grandparents.

Chad's grandmother Bessie taught at Miami area schools for 38 years, and she did not tolerate bad behavior. She made sure Chad stayed out of trouble. Later, as a Bengal, Chad told the *Cincinnati Post* that many people he grew up with got into trouble:

> **If it weren't for football, I'd be one of three places: I'd be dead, I'd be in jail, or what's the third thing? Selling drugs. I guarantee you I could give you 30 names right now of people I grew up with who are dead. We got 'em dead, we got 'em in jail, we got 'em on the street hustling.**

School Days

Even though Bessie was a teacher, she could not get Chad interested in school. The only class he really liked was gym. Sometimes he would skip other classes to attend gym classes over and over. He loved playing football, soccer, basketball, and other sports, but he did not put the same amount of effort into his classwork.

This made high school difficult for Chad, but he took football seriously. At Miami Beach High School, Chad played wide receiver for three years before moving to quarterback his senior year. His cousin, Samari Rolle, also played quarterback there. Rolle and another of Chad's cousins, Keyshawn Johnson, later played in the NFL.

Chad was so fast that one day he **outpaced** assistant football coach Dale Sims while he went out for a long pass. Sims, who had been a track star in college, said no player had ever outrun him before.

Chad's high school years were not easy. During that time, James, who attended many of Chad's games, was murdered. To this day, that crime has not been solved.

Chad's grades were not good enough to get him into a major college. After high school, he attended a small college in Oklahoma. Before he played a single game, however, Chad was thrown off the college team for fighting.

Junior College Star

Chad soon went to live with his mother in California. There he played football for Santa Monica Junior College. At Santa Monica, he met some people who would become important parts of his life. One of them was Charles Collins, who coached the team's receivers. Collins had played professional football in Canada. Chad also met future Pro Bowler—and friend—Steve Smith.

Chad helped Santa Monica score about 40 points a game, but while he excelled on the field, he still struggled in school. Because of his bad grades, Chad sat out the 1998 season. He returned in 1999. That year, however, Chad was arrested for a fight with his girlfriend.

Chad's off-field setbacks frustrated people who cared about Chad, including Collins. Collins finally got through to Chad. He later described their relationship in an interview with ESPN:

CROSS-CURRENTS

Read "Junior College Football" to learn how some troubled athletes are able to work their way to major colleges, Go to page 48. ▶▶

> **"**He was almost to a point where he was not going to be playing football. Pretty much everybody had given up on him, and I was really sick of him. The minute you think he's got it together, he does something else. I almost actually was going to give up on him. But I figured if I gave up on him, he'd either be in jail or not here, as in dead.**"**

Oregon State Star

Coach Collins **recommended** Chad to Coach Dennis Erickson at Oregon State University, a major university. In 2000 Chad worked his way into Oregon State's starting lineup, and finished as the Beavers' leading receiver. He helped the team earn a number four ranking in the nation in the Associated Press poll. Oregon State had never been rated so high.

Some of Chad's biggest catches included a 15-yard touchdown catch in a 31-21 upset of Southern California and a school-record 97-yard touchdown catch against Stanford. In his one season as a Beaver, Chad caught 37 passes for 806 yards and eight touchdowns.

Fans watch an Oregon State football game at Reser Stadium. In 2000 the Beavers finished with an 11-1 record, thanks largely to Chad's 37 catches for 806 yards and eight touchdowns.

Chad closed his Oregon State days with a 74-yard touchdown catch in the Fiesta Bowl. The Beavers blew out Notre Dame 41-9. Before the bowl game, Chad had predicted that Notre Dame's defense would not be fast enough to cover him. He was right.

During that year, NFL **scouts** took notice of Chad, but some wondered if he was a "one-season wonder." They questioned his problems in school, along with his poor performance in a pre-**draft** event called the **scouting combine**.

CROSS-CURRENTS

To learn about another receiver who went from Oregon State to Cincinnati, read "Houshmandzadeh Keeps Bengals Moving." Go to page 48. ▶▶

EARNING HIS STRIPES

O n an April day in 2001, more than 100 friends and family gathered with Chad at his grandmother's house. They were there to watch the NFL draft on television. Chad expected to be drafted early, when NFL teams were still selecting top college players. When he was not picked in the first round, Chad began to get nervous.

Six wide receivers were selected in that first round. The Chicago Bears selected Michigan's David Terrell with the eighth pick. With the very next pick, the Seattle Seahawks took Koren Robinson from North Carolina State. Rod Gardner and Santana Moss were the next to go. The Philadelphia Eagles then took Freddie Mitchell, and Reggie Wayne went to the Indianapolis Colts.

Before the 2001 NFL draft, Chad told ESPN's Mel Kiper, "I'm looking to do big things as a rookie, yet I understand the hard work, discipline and attention to detail that it takes to [succeed in] the NFL."

Early in the second round, the Cleveland Browns selected another wide receiver, Quincy Morgan. Coach Collins, who was at Chad's Liberty City home, noticed Chad was getting upset.

Chad had not done very well in the pre-draft scouting combine, a set of drills college players perform for NFL scouts. Chad ran 40 yards in 4.57 seconds. Scouts would prefer a time closer to 4.4 seconds for wide receivers. Chad said he had slipped at the combine. On draft day, Chad was slipping again, as teams picked other receivers instead of him.

Finally, with the fifth pick of the second round—the 36th pick overall—the Cincinnati Bengals selected Chad. Collins told an ESPN reporter about that moment:

"We looked at each other, and I grabbed him and hugged him, and he just . . . it all came out. All the struggle, all those things that he thought would never happen. They finally came true. It was like, 'Now it's for real.' . . . I'm proud of him."

Path to the Bengals

When the Bengals picked Chad, they already knew more about him than most NFL teams know about their rookies. Bengals assistant coach Bob Bratkowski had served as a coach at the Senior Bowl, a game for top college players, and he had watched Chad.

CROSS-CURRENTS

For some history of the city where the Bengals play, read "The River Keeps Cincinnati Rolling." Go to page 49. ▶▶

In Senior Bowl practices, Bratkowski noticed that no defensive backs could cover Chad. In the game, Chad caught seven passes for 93 yards.

Bratkowski also knew Coach Erickson, Chad's coach at Oregon State. Bratkowski had worked with Erickson for 12 years and trusted Erickson's belief that Chad would do well in the NFL. At that time, Bratkowski worked for the Pittsburgh Steelers, but the Bengals soon hired him—just in time for him to recommend Chad.

Cincinnati had selected Peter Warrick, a wide receiver, in the first round in 2000. The team's coaches were not sure they wanted to take another receiver in the first round in 2001. When no other teams selected Chad in that first round, Bratkowski convinced the Bengal coaches to take him in the second round. Bratkowski talked about that moment:

> **❝I said this was a guy who could give us something we didn't have here: an ability to change a game and to win one-on-one matchups.❞**

Chad wasn't the only member of the Oregon State team to be drafted. Coach Erickson recommended receiver T.J. Houshmandzadeh,

Chad is good friends with teammate T.J. Houshmandzadeh, shown here catching a pass. "We're like family," says Houshmandzadeh. "I can say a lot of things to Chad that other guys can't, both in football and other things."

and the Bengals listened. They selected Houshmandzadeh in the seventh round.

Both receivers eventually would make the Pro Bowl. The Bengals' web site calls that year's draft "the greatest in Bengals history."

Rookie Moves

Rookies need time to learn how to play in the NFL, so it would take time for the new players to help the Bengals. Cincinnati had struggled for years, but Chad did not mind being drafted by the Bengals. He thought he could change things. After all, Oregon State didn't win many games before Chad had arrived.

Warrick was the team's leading receiver, so Chad had to work for a spot on the Bengals' offense. He made his first two NFL catches in

Chad makes a diving catch during an October 2002 game against the Tennessee Titans. During the 2002 season Chad emerged as one of the AFC's most exciting wide receivers. His 16.9 average yards per catch ranked fourth in the NFL.

a September loss to the San Diego Chargers. One of those catches was his first NFL touchdown.

In October, Chad began to hit his stride. He caught five passes for 68 yards during a game against the Cleveland Browns. In the third quarter of that game, however, Chad was injured. X-rays showed he had broken his collarbone. He would miss the next four games.

Chad finished the year with 28 catches for 329 yards—not bad for a rookie who had missed four games of the season. The Bengals, however, finished the season 6-10. Chad had expected more.

Turning Point

In Chad's second season, the Bengals began to expect more from him. Chad said a key moment in his NFL career came in 2002, during his second season. After starting the season with four straight losses, the Bengals faced a strong Indianapolis Colts team.

Surprisingly, Cincinnati trailed by just one touchdown late in the game—and they were still driving down the field. With 31 seconds left, Chad broke free. Bengals quarterback Jon Kitna spotted him. He threw the ball to Chad, but Chad couldn't catch the pass. To make matters worse, the ball actually hit him on the head! It then fell into the hands of a Colts player for an **interception**.

The Bengals had lost another game. Chad thought he had cost the team a win. In the locker room, he was very upset. Kitna decided to talk to him. Later, Kitna recalled what he said:

> **"You have the opportunity not just to be good. You can be a superstar. But this is a defining moment. You're going to go one of two ways. You're going to decide it's not going to matter to you—it's not worth it—and you'll be out of the league in a couple of years. Or, you're going to go the other way and be a superstar."**

Chad took those words to heart. Before the star could emerge, hard work was needed. Chad began arriving at practice earlier, and he started doing extra running. He even worked with the **scout team** during practice.

Chad also became good friends with Kitna. He appreciated how Kitna taught him to be a pro:

> **❝I didn't have anyone in that locker room to learn from. Nobody taught me how to be a professional. We didn't have strong veteran leadership, so I had to learn it on my own. Kitna was the first guy to set me straight.❞**

Making Strides

Now that a teammate had helped show him the way, Chad's hard work began to pay off. Late in 2002, Chad had three straight 100-yard games against division rivals Baltimore, Cleveland, and Pittsburgh. Against Cleveland, he scored the team's longest touchdown of the season: a 72-yard pass from Kitna. Chad also led the team in catches for the season, with 69.

At the end of the year, Coach Bratkowski challenged Chad to improve in 2003. The *Cincinnati Post* reported what Bratkowski told the receiver:

> **❝I told him, 'You're going to have to clean up a lot of the sloppy things that you do in your game.' Becoming an elite receiver is an achievable thing if he'll do that. . . . He needs to push himself hard at times.❞**

The Bengals finished 2-14 in 2002, but Chad was not discouraged. He followed his coach's advice. He attended an offseason seminar with NFL star Deion Sanders and soaked up advice from the All-Pro cornerback. Chad said that Deion showed him he could be one of the best receivers in the NFL.

The Guarantee

In 2003, Chad believed in himself, in the new Bengals coach Marvin Lewis, and in the entire Bengals team. He was so confident that he told the media he guaranteed the Bengals would beat a strong Kansas City team. The Kansas City Chiefs came to Cincinnati with an 8-0 record.

CROSS-CURRENTS

Read "Coach Marvin Lewis" to learn about the African-American coach hired by the Bengals before the 2003 season. Go to page 50. ▶▶

A Denver Broncos defensive back can't keep up as Chad catches a pass during the first game of the 2003 season. By the end of 2003, Chad had established himself as one of the league's best receivers.

Even though the Bengals were just 4-5, Chad thought they would win at home.

In the game, Chad caught seven passes for 74 yards. Warrick had an even bigger game, with a punt return for a touchdown and six catches for 114 yards—including a 77-yard touchdown. Running back Rudi Johnson also ran 165 yards for the Bengals. With these great performances, the Bengals pulled off a 24-19 win.

After the game, Chad had second thoughts about his guarantee. He realized it put extra pressure on his team, and some of the Chiefs players thought Chad wasn't respecting them. Chad apologized, but said he was glad the Bengals had won:

"That's having my back. They didn't leave me hanging in the wind, and I didn't want to leave them hanging in the wind.**"**

Watching Every Move

That season, the Bengals' lounge featured a new addition: a pillow and blankets on a couch. The pillow and blankets were Chad's. Chad decided to sleep in the Bengal lounge because he spent so much time watching videos of the games there. Chad studied his performance, he watched his opponents, and he planned new moves.

Thanks to his great 2003 season—90 catches for 1,355 yards and 10 touchdowns—Chad was selected for the AFC's Pro Bowl team. During the Pro Bowl, Chad caught five passes, including a 90-yard touchdown.

The hard work paid off. Chad set a Bengal season record of 1,355 receiving yards. He led the AFC in that category. He also scored ten touchdowns. Because of his great season, Chad earned his first Pro Bowl trip.

The Bengals also improved. The Kansas City victory moved the Bengals into a tie for first place in the AFC North. At one point the Bengals had a win-loss record of 7-5. But they lost three of their last four games to finish with an 8-8 record, just missing a spot in the playoffs.

New Quarterback

While Kitna was helping the Bengals improve, another quarterback was waiting his turn. In 2003, Cincinnati drafted Carson Palmer with the first pick in the NFL draft. Palmer had earned the Heisman Trophy as college football's best player in 2002. In 2003, he was given time to learn about the NFL while he backed up Kitna. In 2004, the Bengals decided to make Palmer the starter.

Chad helped the new quarterback do well his first year. In 2004, Chad again finished as the leading receiver in the AFC, with 1,274 yards. His 95 catches ranked him third in the NFL, and he made the Pro Bowl for the second time. Chad told the *Sporting News* he wanted to be the best receiver ever:

"That's the whole point. Otherwise, why play the game?"

Chad was doing well individually, but the team failed to make the playoffs. They did, however, finish 8-8 again in 2004. The Bengals were getting better. In 2005, the Bengals finally broke through.

TIME TO CELEBRATE

In 2005, the Bengals were a much-improved team. By mid-December, the Bengals had a 10-3 record. With three games left to play, the Bengals could clinch the AFC North Division title if they could beat the Lions in Detroit. This would put Cincinnati into the NFL playoffs for the first time in 15 years.

The team turned to Chad for help. Chad was considered the best receiver in the AFC, and he didn't let the team down. In the game against Detroit, he delivered a career-best 11 catches.

In the first quarter, Chad beat Pro Bowl cornerback Dre Bly to the corner of the end zone. Chad then hauled in a one-yard touchdown pass to put the Bengals up 17-0. Oddly enough, Chad didn't celebrate this touchdown with a dance. After the game,

The Cincinnati Bengals were a much-improved team in 2005. With Chad leading the AFC in receiving yardage, the Bengals finished with an 11-5 record and earned the team's first playoff spot in 15 years.

he told the Associated Press he did not want to take focus away from the game:

> **"This game was too important. I just wanted to play it safe because we needed a win."**

Chad finished with 99 receiving yards, and the Bengals cruised to a 41-17 win. This gave the team its first division title since 1990. Chad was a key part of many of Cincinnati's 11 wins in 2005.

Spotlight on Chad

Chad's great performance, along with his touchdown celebrations, drew national attention that season. Chad, whose number is 85, kept a checklist that asked, "Who covered 85 in 2005?" Each week Chad gave a mark either to himself or to his opponent, a defensive back. The defensive back only earned a mark if he was able to cover Chad. At the end of the 16-game regular season, Chad had 15 marks.

Chad runs with the football after making a catch against the Indianapolis Colts, November 20, 2005. Although Chad had one of his best games of the season—eight catches for 189 yards—the Colts won the high-scoring game, 45-37.

According to Chad, the only player to cover him had been Cleveland Browns cornerback Leigh Bodden.

The Bengals started the 2005 season with four straight wins. In the second game, the Minnesota Vikings were having a hard time covering Chad. He had speed, and his hours of viewing videos helped him find weaknesses in defensive backs.

In that game, Chad caught a 70-yard touchdown on the second offensive play. Quarterback Carson Palmer told NFL.com that Chad's big play helped both the short passing game and the running game:

> **"When a guy gets open that early, it definitely puts fear into their hearts."**

Chad finished the Vikings game with seven catches for 139 yards.

The following week, Chad caught just three passes against the tough Chicago Bears' defense—but two of those catches were touchdowns.

After his second touchdown against Chicago, Chad did a dance inspired by "Riverdance," an Irish music and dance show. Chad enjoys watching musicals. He had seen a television commercial for "Riverdance," and he decided to try the dance. After the touchdown, he moved to the back of the end zone. He put his hands on his hips, lifted his knees, and pointed his toes. Then he kicked up his heels.

The Dancing Receiver

That dance was just one of many touchdown celebrations. Chad worked hard during the week to prepare for games. When he scored a touchdown, he wanted to let loose and have fun.

After scoring a touchdown against the Indianapolis Colts, he ran up to one of the Ben-Gal cheerleaders, got down on one knee, and asked, "Will you marry me?" He was just having fun, of course! After another touchdown, this one against the Buffalo Bills, Chad passed out presents to lucky fans in the first few rows.

In an interview with *The Sporting News*, Chad talked about his celebrations:

CROSS-CURRENTS

Read "Celebrating a Score" to learn about how some other NFL players have celebrated their touchdowns. Go to page 51. ▶▶

❝Usually, what makes it fun is I'll give you a hint of what I'm going to do each week. It makes you want to say, 'OK, let's see what Chad has for us this week.' It's funny, the players in the NFL every week, they always ask me in pre-game, 'What have you got for us?' Even the players can't wait to see it.**❞**

In another memorable TD celebration, Chad performed **cardiopulmonary resuscitation**, or CPR, on a football. He pumped on the ball with his hands, like rescuers do when they try to save someone who has stopped breathing. After a touchdown against Baltimore, Chad acted like he was a golfer. He used an orange end zone marker to putt the football. After a touchdown against the Tennessee Titans, Chad took over a television camera and pretended to film players.

After a touchdown in 2006, Chad even did the **chicken dance** and moved his arms like chicken wings. Chad also led the World's Largest Chicken Dance during Cincinnati's Oktoberfest celebration. In 2007, Chad jumped into the "Dawg Pound," a section of fans at Cleveland. The fans dumped drinks on him.

Chad didn't just dance. In 2006, he also asked to be called by the nickname "Ocho Cinco"—"eight five" in Spanish. Before one game, the back of his jersey said "Ocho Cinco," but he later took off the nickname to reveal his own name. Chad was still fined by the NFL for a uniform violation. In 2006, Chad explained his nickname during a press conference:

❝My name isn't Chad no more. We're celebrating Spanish history month in the month of October in the NFL. Ocho Cinco from now on. Anybody that writes about whatever I say today, you call me 'Ocho Cinco.' Do not say Chad.**❞**

The Playoffs

Chad and the Bengals had plenty of fun in 2005. After the first four wins, the Bengals won six of their final nine games to win the AFC North Division with an 11-5 record.

Chad finished as the AFC leader in receiving yards, with 1,432 yards. His former junior college teammate, Steve Smith of the

Carolina Panthers, finished first in the National Football Conference (NFC), with 1,563 yards.

In the playoffs, the Bengals faced the Pittsburgh Steelers with confidence. The Bengals had defeated the Steelers a month earlier in Pittsburgh, 38-31. The playoff game would be fought in Cincinnati.

On the Bengals' second offensive play of the game, Palmer completed a long pass to receiver Chris Henry. On that play, however, Steelers defensive tackle Kimo von Oelhoffen hit Palmer low after Palmer threw the pass. Palmer injured his knee and could not play the rest of the game. Jon Kitna took over, and the Bengals led 17-14 at halftime.

CROSS-CURRENTS

For information about Cincinnati's 1982 and 1989 appearances in the NFL's biggest game, read "The Bengals in the Super Bowl." Go to page 51. ▶▶

A fan holds up an "Ocho-Cinco" sign during a Bengals game. "I don't know why the NFL is worried about [my] touchdown celebrations," Chad said in 2006. "[W]hen I come up with a new celebration, the fans love it."

In the locker room at halftime, Chad felt dehydrated, and he took in lots of fluids. Chad also argued with Coach Lewis and the other coaches because he wanted the ball more. Later, Bengals receivers coach Hue Jackson said Chad often doesn't feel as if he is helping the team if he doesn't catch passes:

> **He thinks he can carry his team on his back. His medicine is the ball. Giving him the football is a shot of energy. Not the media, not his teammates. The ball. That's who he is. That's his core. You never want to take that away from him.**

In the second half, the Steelers rallied for a 31-17 win. The Bengals had finished ahead of the Steelers in the regular season, but

The Bengals play from deep in their own territory during the January 8, 2006, playoff game against the Pittsburgh Steelers. (Chad is spread wide to the right.) The Steelers won the game, 31-17.

the Steelers had taken their revenge. Chad finished the game with four catches for 59 yards. The Steelers went on to win the Super Bowl over the Seattle Seahawks.

Distraction?

Even after Palmer was injured, the Bengals thought they should have defeated Pittsburgh. Some coaches thought Chad got too carried away at halftime. They thought his arguments with the coaches distracted the team.

Chad is an emotional player. His emotions push him to be better, but they also can cause him to overreact. Some coaches, teammates, and opponents have questioned Chad's need to celebrate touchdowns and talk during games.

At times, Coach Lewis has asked Chad to hold back. He said Chad's fun could become a distraction. The team can be penalized, and sometimes Chad is fined. Chad has toned it down at times, but he still likes to celebrate. He told *The Sporting News* he tries to share his joy with the fans:

> **All I do is make the game fun and interesting again. And all of those people who may be old school and really don't like that stuff—in the back of their minds every Sunday, they can't wait to see what I'm going to do either. I've brought excitement back to the game. And I do it in a positive way. I'm never negative. I'm never degrading any opponent.**

Carson's Comeback

Carson Palmer's knee injury was very serious. He had torn two **ligaments**, and many experts thought he would miss games in 2006. Palmer, however, worked hard to become healthy, and he started in the 2006 opening game against Kansas City. The Bengals won that game 23-10.

The team went on to win the next two games, but then it struggled. The Bengals lost five of their next six games.

Chad and Palmer, however, still led the offense. In a November loss against the San Diego Chargers, Chad set a team record with 260 yards in one game. The previous record had been set in 1988,

Chad greets Bengals quarterback Carson Palmer (number 9) on the sidelines during Cincinnati's 2006 training camp. Palmer came back from a serious injury to throw 28 touchdown passes—seven to Chad—during the 2006 season.

when Eddie Brown had 216 yards. Chad beat the Charger defense all day. He made 11 catches and caught two touchdown passes, one for 51 yards and the other for 74 yards.

Still, the Chargers rallied from a score of 28-7 at halftime to beat the Bengals 49-41. LaDainian Tomlinson scored four touchdowns for the Chargers. Chad told the Associated Press the loss was frustrating:

"There are a lot of unhappy people. There are reasons why we lost today."

The next week, in a game against New Orleans, Chad caught six passes for 190 yards and three touchdowns. He played well, even though he was hurting with a leg injury. On a 60-yard touchdown, he limped into the end zone. The Bengals won the game, 31-16, to improve to 5-5.

In those two games, Chad had 450 yards. That is the most receiving yards in two consecutive games in NFL history! Chad told NFL.com it is important to be good every week:

"I'm trying to be as consistent as possible, trying to make sure I do all I can to make sure we come up out of this hole and make this run."

At the end of the 2006 season, the Bengals again had a chance to make the playoffs. However, they lost their final game to the Pittsburgh Steelers. Pittsburgh won, 23-17, in overtime. Cincinnati finished 8-8 and just missed the playoffs.

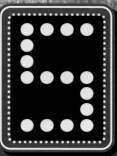

FUTURE HALL OF FAMER?

I n 2007, Chad didn't waste any time before he started having fun. The Bengals opened the season at Paul Brown Stadium in a game against their AFC rivals, the Baltimore Ravens. The game was played on a Monday night. This was another chance for Chad and the Bengals to grab the national spotlight.

Although the NFL plays most of its games on Sunday afternoons, there are some night games. Monday night games typically receive the most attention. With the stadium lights shining in Cincinnati, Chad planned the celebration that would become one of the best known of his career—the one featuring his famous "H.O.F. 20??" jacket.

Chad prepares himself before a 2007 game against the Baltimore Ravens. The star wide receiver had another great year, catching 93 passes for a career-best 1,440 yards and eight touchdowns. However, the Bengals stumbled to a 7-9 record that season.

Now he just had to score a touchdown. Chad took care of that in the first quarter. He ran past the Ravens' defensive backs into the tiger-striped end zone and hauled in a 39-yard touchdown pass from Carson Palmer. After he scored, Chad put his finger up to tell fans to wait just a minute.

CROSS-CURRENTS

To learn more about Chad's quarterback with the Bengals, check out "Heisman Winner Carson Palmer." Go to page 52. ▶▶

Chad jogged to the sidelines. On the sidelines, teammate T.J. Houshmandzadeh put a jacket on Chad's back. Chad made sure that as many fans as possible could see the lettering on his jacket—"Future H.O.F. 20??" The 66,093 fans roared their approval, and many laughed with Chad. They know he likes to have fun after touchdowns.

The jacket's suggestion that Chad would make the Pro Football Hall of Fame in coming years wasn't entirely the product of his cocky style. Only the very best NFL players make the Hall of Fame. With five straight Pro Bowl appearances and his many career records, Chad will have a good chance of making it into the Hall of Fame.

In that season-opening game, Chad finished with five catches for 95 yards, and the Bengals won 27-20.

Horsepower

A few months before that game, Chad pulled a stunt that fans everywhere watched. Chad planned a race against a horse named Restore the Roar. For a week Chad insisted he would win the race.

The race was held on a sunny May day on the grass race course at Cincinnati's River Downs. Chad received a big head start and then accelerated quickly on the outside edge of the course. The 8,000 fans at the track cheered. Restore the Roar gained on Chad late, but Chad charged under the wire first. He had won! Chad said once he found out he had a 100-meter head start, he expected to win.

Jockey Patti Cooksey rode the horse. She told a *Cincinnati Enquirer* reporter she was impressed with Chad's speed:

❝He's quick. He's a fast man. That was phenomenal. When I looked over at him, all I could see were his legs; they looked like a windmill. He was a blur. I was beat bad.❞

Chad walks onto the track at River Downs, Cincinnati, for a charitable event, June 9, 2007. "It's all for fun," Chad said before racing—and beating—a horse. "The important thing is raising money to help those in need."

After winning the race, Chad rode a horse into the winner's circle. Then Chad challenged other top sports stars. He said he wanted to fight top boxer Floyd Mayweather, play basketball against NBA All-Stars Kobe Bryant or LeBron James, or race a car against NASCAR's Jeff Gordon. Of course Chad was just kidding around.

The race was not only fun; it also helped raise money for a charity, Feed The Children. Chad works with this charity to help support a school in Africa.

A Child at Heart

Many of Chad's favorite charities involve children, and he likes to have fun while helping these charities. In 2007, he opened his performance check list to fan voting. The voting was sponsored

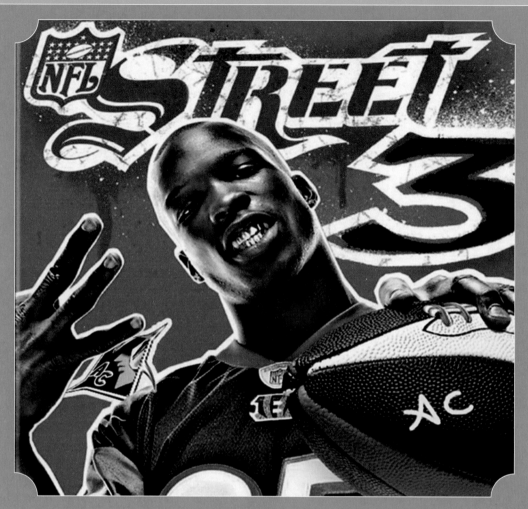

Because of his immense popularity, Chad Johnson was featured on the cover of the video game NFL Street 3. He has also done ads for GoDaddy.com and Reebok and has been featured in NFL Network and *ESPN Sportscenter* commercials.

by the deodorant Degree Men, a product for which Chad has done commercials. For each vote, Degree Men made a donation of 8.5 cents to Feed the Children. Chad said he hoped to raise $85,000 for the charity:

"My checklist has always given me extra motivation. But the opportunity to help needy kids around the world

increases my drive. I had the unique opportunity to tour Kenya in the spring, and it really opened my eyes. I hope the fans will get behind the checklist this season because Degree Men has made it so simple to help these kids. **"**

Chad's success and celebrations have made him very popular. He has done ads for GoDaddy.com and Reebok and has been featured in NFL Network commercials. Chad also appeared in funny advertisements for *ESPN Sportscenter* and was on the box cover for the video game NFL Street 3. Chad talked about the cover appearance:

"This is a big honor to be selected for the cover for NFL Street 3 since street football was the first step to learning our moves for our pro careers. I really like this game, and it is so much fun to play with all the new airborne moves you can do now. **"**

In his spare time, Chad sometimes attends high school football games in Cincinnati and Special Olympics events. The Special Olympics provide sports training and hold events for people with disabilities. Coach Lewis said young Special Olympics athletes love meeting Chad. The coach also said Chad is trying to help people:

"He's a live-for-the-moment guy, but he has become more aware of big picture things. Relationships, financial things, things he can do off the field. He realizes he doesn't have it all figured out. **"**

At Home

While Chad likes to dance on the field, he prefers to relax off the field. Chad enjoys spending time at home, and he usually goes to bed early. Chad doesn't drink or smoke.

On off days, Chad likes shopping for CDs and DVDs. He enjoys a wide variety of music, from new rap hits to songs that were popular in the 1940s. Chad also likes jewelry.

Chad is not married and has four children. His children live with their mothers in Florida and California, but Chad spends some weekends with them. Sometimes he brings his children to games. He told *Sports Illustrated* that he would like to spend more time with them:

"My job keeps me from being there as much as I would like. But what I do right now is for them in the future. I don't think I'm the father I need to be right now. It doesn't really bother me that much because once I'm done, I'll have all the time in the world with them. I've lost a little time. I know I'm missing something valuable—valuable moments in their life."

Chad likes to drive, and he has 12 cars and trucks. Still, Chad's focus is on football. The Bengals now give players DVDs of games to take home. Chad enjoys playing these DVDs over and over. He watches himself and his opponents to improve his play.

Chad also enjoys talking to Bengal coaches about plays. Coach Lewis said some of Chad's ideas have helped the team:

"Chad has broken down the barrier between players and coaches. He is helping us turn the corner that way. He knows we're all in this together. There is no class system with him. No wall of separation."

Bengals Come Up Short

Chad and the coaches worked together in 2007. The team won many home games, but they struggled during games on the road.

Despite the losses, Chad put together another top season. He broke his own single-season record with 1,440 receiving yards. Chad also continued to be consistent. He caught at least one pass in every game. In fact, through 2007, he had caught at least one pass in 92 straight games. He led the NFL in first downs by a receiver, with 76 first downs, two more than New England's Randy Moss. He had five 100-yard games, giving him a team-record of 26 100-yard games in his career.

In a loss to the Cleveland Browns, Chad had 11 catches for 209 yards and two touchdowns. The 209 yards were the most yards gained by any receiver in a single game in the NFL during 2007.

T.J. Houshmandzadeh (bottom) gets a hug from Chad after scoring a touchdown during the 2008 Pro Bowl. After another strong season in 2007, Chad was invited to go to the Pro Bowl for the fifth time.

Chad is also setting Bengals career records. In the Cleveland game, he became the team's all-time leader in receiving yards, passing Bengals great Isaac Curtis. At the end of the year, he had 8,365 career yards. In a November game against the Tennessee Titans, Chad became the all-time leader in catches for the Bengals. Through 2007, he had 559 catches.

CROSS-CURRENTS

Read "The AFC North Division" to find out about Cincinnati's main rivals: Pittsburgh, Baltimore, and Cleveland. Go to page 53. ▶▶

Uncertain Future

Despite all the catches, individual success is not enough for Chad. He wants to play on a top team, and he wants to win a Super Bowl. In 2007, the Bengals again

"I'd rather be hated for who I am, than loved for who I'm not."
-Chad Johnson

i am what i am

Rbk

Chad Johnson—shown here in an enormous advertisement—holds many Bengals records. These include most career catches, most career receiving yards, and most receiving yards in a season. His 49 career touchdowns are third on the team's all-time list.

did not do well enough to make the playoffs. Chad was frustrated, and he asked to be traded after the season. Chad threatened to **hold out** and not play if he did not get traded.

Sports Illustrated ranked Chad's possible holdout as one of the top ten offseason NFL stories of 2008. Chad skipped some voluntary workouts in the spring. If he were to sit out the season, he would not be paid his $3 million salary. The Washington Redskins and Philadelphia Eagles expressed interest in Chad, hoping the Bengals would consider trading their star receiver.

Some experts said Chad wanted to hold out because he wants to be paid more money. Before the 2006 season, Chad signed a six-year **contract** worth $35.5 million. Bengals Coach Marvin Lewis told *Sports Illustrated* that the team would not let Chad out of that contract:

> **We've made it clear what the stance is. It's not going to change, today or in August, whenever. You cannot allow a player to get up on his high chair with four years left on his contract and demand to get out. If you do that, you set a terrible example for the rest of your team, and we won't do that.**

Chad and Football

Whether it's for the Bengals or for another team, Chad probably still has many years left catching passes, scoring touchdowns, and celebrating. Former Pro Bowl cornerback Deion Sanders once talked about Chad's love of football with *The Sporting News*:

> **I think he could be misunderstood at times because of his passion for the game. He just wants to dominate and win on every play.**

On the field, Chad's passion has helped him succeed, and he has helped the Bengals improve.

Off the field, Chad is finding ways to help young people in Cincinnati and around the world. Chad loves to celebrate each success, on and off the field. Just watch him!

Paul Brown Stadium

In 2000, the Cincinnati Bengals unveiled their new home, Paul Brown Stadium.

The stadium was named after the Bengals' founder, Paul Brown. It is located on Cincinnati's riverfront and encloses an area of more than 40 acres. The stadium's field is made of an artificial surface called FieldTurf. Huge scoreboards with large video screens are behind each of the field's end zones.

The stadium is nicknamed "The Jungle" to match the theme of the team's name, and the song "Welcome to the Jungle" is played before every kick-off. The walls of the stadium's lower level are painted with Bengal stripes and jungle scenes. Most fans in the lower level stand and cheer for the entire game.

In 2007, Paul Brown Stadium was the only football stadium to make a list of America's favorite 150 buildings and structures. The Bengals' home was listed at 101.

The Bengals played their first two seasons at Nippert Stadium, where today the University of Cincinnati Bearcats play. In 1970, the Bengals moved to Riverfront Stadium. They shared that stadium with baseball's Cincinnati Reds until 1999, when they moved to Paul Brown Stadium

A record crowd of 64,006 fans turned out for the Bengals' first regular season game at Paul Brown Stadium. Now the team regularly draws more than 66,000 fans. (Go back to page 6.) ◀◀

Chad has scored many touchdowns at Cincinnati's Paul Brown Stadium. The field, which opened in 2000, is named for the team's founder. Fans have nicknamed the stadium "the Jungle," in reference to the team's nickname.

Orange-and-Black Attack

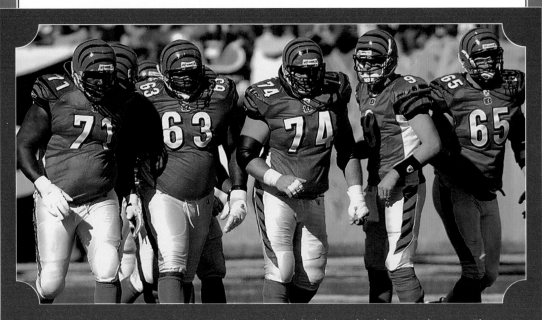

The Bengals' uniforms feature tiger stripes on the helmets, shoulders, and pants. The team occasionally wears these orange jerseys. For most home games, the team wears black-and-orange jerseys. On the road the Bengals typically wear white-and-orange jerseys.

The Cincinnati Bengals are named after the Bengal tiger, an impressive animal. The Bengal tiger lives in Asia and can grow to weigh up to 500 pounds in the wild.

The Bengals' helmets and uniforms feature the tiger's stripes. The team's orange helmets have black tiger stripes, the jerseys have tiger-striped patterns on the shoulders, and the pants have tiger stripes on the sides. Sometimes the players wear black pants with stripes, and sometimes they wear white pants with stripes.

Before the 1981 season, the Bengals' helmets featured the word "Bengals," but team founder Paul Brown wanted a helmet that would stand out. In 1981, the name was taken off the helmets, and six black tiger stripes were placed on both sides. That year, the Bengals went to the Super Bowl for the first time. Many fans believed the new stripes brought the team luck, and the stripes have stayed on the helmets ever since.

Today the Bengals choose from three different jerseys: a white jersey with black numbers and black sleeves, a black jersey with white numbers and orange sleeves, and an orange jersey with white numbers and orange sleeves. All three jerseys, of course, have tiger stripes on the shoulders.

The team's current logo is an orange "B" with black stripes. (Go back to page 9.) ◀◀

Junior College Football

Many top high school football players go on to attend large four-year universities such as the University of Florida, Ohio State University, and the University of Southern California. Not all top players, however, attend these types of colleges right after high school.

Some players struggle with their schoolwork in high school, so they are not prepared for the classes at major universities. Other players are not quite large or muscular enough to play for these universities. Junior colleges give players a chance to improve. Players who struggled in school can improve their grades, and players who were too small can work to increase their muscle mass.

The top junior college football teams of 2007 were Butler Community College in Kansas and Mississippi Gulf Coast Community College. The National Junior College Athletic Association releases polls of top teams and keeps statistics of top players. It selects an All-American team and also offers bowl games for its teams.

After a few years at a junior college, top players can go on to play for major colleges. NFL stars Chad Johnson and Steve Smith are just a few of the players who played junior college football. In 2008, NFL teams drafted 12 players who had played football at a junior college. (Go back to page 14.) ◄◄

Houshmandzadeh Keeps Bengals Moving

When the Bengals scouted Chad Johnson in college, they also noticed his Oregon State teammate T.J. Houshmandzadeh. Like Chad, T.J. also plays receiver.

The Bengals selected Chad in the second round of the 2001 draft and took T.J. in the seventh round. In 2007, T.J. and Chad both played in the Pro Bowl.

T.J. is from Barstow, California. He is 6-feet, 1-inch tall and weighs 199 pounds. T.J. is very strong and good at catching short passes, which help the Bengals continue to drive down the field. Chad, on the other hand, is known for catching long passes.

Eric Yarber coached T.J. and Chad at Oregon State. When scouts watched Chad, Yarber asked them to watch T.J. as well. He told the Bengals that drafting T.J. in the seventh round would be a steal. Yarber thinks T.J.'s strength and Chad's speed test the opponent's defenses.

In 2007, T.J. scored at least one touchdown in each of the Bengals' first eight games. That is the most games in a row any Bengal has scored a touchdown. At the end of the season, he tied Wes Welker for most catches in the NFL, with 112 catches. Those 112 catches are also the most catches made by a Bengal in a single season. (Go back to page 15.) ◄◄

The River Keeps Cincinnati Rolling

Cincinnati sits on the banks of the Ohio River. Because of its location, the city developed as a way station for settlers moving west in the late 18th century. The city was named Losantiville in 1789, but it was renamed Cincinnati a year later. The name honors Roman citizen-soldier Lucius Quinctius Cincinnatus.

Cincinnati's history has been tied to the river. Easy shipping helped the city become a world leader in pork-packing. In the mid-19th century, it was nicknamed "Porkopolis," and in 1852, more than 8,000 steamboats were based in Cincinnati.

Cincinnati prospered after the Civil War. Its population grew to 200,000 people, and it briefly became the country's largest city. Around this time, two city landmarks were unveiled: the John R. Roebling suspension bridge and the Tyler Davidson Fountain.

Today, about 330,000 people live in Cincinnati, and the city is a leader in the production of machine tools, playing cards, soaps, and jet engines.

People in Cincinnati continue to flock to the river for fun activities. In recent years, Cincinnati has committed more than $2 billion to improve existing buildings or build new structures in the downtown and riverfront areas. These new structures include the National Underground Railroad Freedom Center and stadiums for the Bengals and the Cincinnati Reds baseball team.
(Go back to page 18.) ◀◀

This view of Cincinnati shows several of the city's bridges over the Ohio River. At one time, Cincinnati had a population of more than 500,000. Today the population is about 330,000, making Cincinnati the third-largest city in Ohio.

Coach Marvin Lewis

In 2002, the Cincinnati Bengals were struggling. They finished the season with a 2-14 record—the worst record in the team's history. Then the Bengals hired Marvin Lewis as their head coach.

Lewis turned the team around in his very first season as coach. He guided Cincinnati to an 8-8 record in 2003, and he finished second to New England coach Bill Belichick in the vote for NFL Coach of the Year. In 2005, Lewis led the Bengals to their first division title since 1990.

The hiring of Lewis marked a change in the Bengals' hiring practices. Bengals President Mike Brown typically hired coaches who had previous ties to the Bengals. The coaches had been former Bengals players or assistant coaches. Lewis, however, had no Bengal ties.

Before joining the Bengals, Lewis had a great coaching record. He coached the defense for the 2000 Super Bowl Champion Baltimore Ravens. In that season, Lewis's Baltimore defense set the NFL record for fewest points allowed in a 16-game season, with 165 points.

Lewis became the eighth African American to be named an NFL head coach and the first African-American head coach in Bengal history. His hiring marked a small step in racial healing in Cincinnati. The city had experienced race riots after a 2001 shooting of a black man by white police officers.

Lewis has been active in the Cincinnati community. He averages about 50 public appearances a year. Lewis also launched the Marvin Lewis Community Fund, a fund that supports programs that educate and inspire the region's young people. (Go back to page 22.) ◀◀

Cincinnati head coach Marvin Lewis gained a reputation for building strong defenses with the Pittsburgh Steelers (1992-1995) and Baltimore Ravens (1996-2001). In his first five seasons as the Bengals' head coach, the team won 42 games and lost 38.

Celebrating a Score

Chad Johnson puts on some of the game's most colorful touchdown celebrations, but Chad was not the first NFL player to celebrate when he scored.

In 1973, Kansas City Chiefs receiver Elmo Wright ran in place and then spiked the ball after catching a touchdown. He was soon followed by Billy "White Shoes" Johnson. In the 1970s, while playing for the Houston Oilers, Johnson danced the "Funky Chicken" after making touchdowns. In 2004, the *Washington Post* rated his celebration as the best of all-time.

At Green Bay's Lambeau Field, Packers' players leap into the stands after scoring. This jump is called the Lambeau Leap. In the 1980s, the Washington Redskins receivers started the "Fun Bunch." The receivers would leap together for a group high-five.

Dallas Cowboys receiver Butch Johnson used to act as if his hands were a cowboy's guns. He would fire away and then blow pretend smoke off his fingers. That celebration was called the "California Quake." The Atlanta Falcons of the late 1990s added the "Dirty Bird," another birdlike dance

Before Chad, the most famous Bengal celebration was the "Ickey Shuffle." Fullback Ickey Woods would dance to his left and then to his right before spiking the ball. The celebration was made famous in 1988, the year the Bengals made it to the Super Bowl. (Go back to page 29.) ◀◀

The Bengals in the Super Bowl

The Cincinnati Bengals' history goes back to 1968, when the team played its first season. The team was founded by Paul Brown. Brown, now a member of the Pro Football Hall of Fame, coached the Bengals for many years. Before starting the Bengals, Brown had coached the Cleveland Browns to three NFL championships.

The Cincinnati Bengals have never won a Super Bowl. The team, however, did make it to the Super Bowl game twice in the 1980s. Oddly enough, the Bengals lost both of their Super Bowl games to the San Francisco 49ers and their star quarterback, Joe Montana.

In the playoffs in 1981, the Bengals defeated the San Diego Chargers, 27-7, to win the American Football Conference championship for the first time. The game was played in Cincinnati, and the weather was very cold. Temperatures were –9° Fahrenheit (–22° Celsius), with a wind chill of –59°F (–51°C).

In the team's first Super Bowl game against San Francisco, Bengals quarterback Ken Anderson led a rally in the second half. The rally came up short, however, and the Bengals lost 26-21.

In 1988, quarterback Boomer Esiason led the Bengals to their second AFC Championship. Esiason, the NFL's Most Valuable Player that season, led a top offense under Coach Sam Wyche. In the Super Bowl, however, the 49ers scored a winning touchdown with just 34 seconds left. The 49ers won 20-16. (Go back to page 31.) ◀◀

Heisman Winner Carson Palmer

Since becoming the Bengals' starting quarterback during the 2004 season, Carson Palmer has set many team records. A former number-one pick in the NFL draft, Carson has passed for more than 100 touchdowns during his career.

Chad Johnson is not the only star on the Bengals. Quarterback Carson Palmer has helped the Bengals' offense become one of the top offenses in the NFL.

In college, Palmer played for the University of Southern California (USC). He threw for more than 11,000 yards and 72 touchdowns during his career. As a senior, his 3,942 yards passing and 33 touchdowns earned him the Heisman Trophy, an award given to the nation's top college football player.

In 2003, the Bengals chose Palmer with the first pick in the NFL draft. This 6-foot, 5-inch, 230-pound quarterback set many team records in his first four seasons as a starter. Palmer holds the Bengals' record for most touchdown passes in a game, with six. He holds single-season records for most completions (373), passing yards (4,131), and touchdown passes (32).

Palmer suffered a bad knee injury in the 2005 playoffs. Through hard work, he was able to play the following year. That year, he made the Pro Bowl and was chosen as the game's Most Valuable Player. In 2007, he was the only NFL quarterback to not miss an offensive play all year.

Palmer is originally from Mission Viejo, California. With his wife Shaelyn, he established the Carson Palmer Foundation in 2004. The foundation supports charities in Southern California and Cincinnati and helps abused and abandoned children. (Go back to page 38.) ◀◀

The AFC North Division

The Cincinnati Bengals play in the AFC, which consists of the North, South, East, and West Divisions. The Bengals play in the AFC North. Other teams in this division are the Baltimore Ravens, the Cleveland Browns, and the Pittsburgh Steelers. These teams play each other twice a year and often have heated rivalries.

Pittsburgh has enjoyed the most NFL success. In the 1970s, Pittsburgh won four Super Bowls. Their defense was called the "Steel Curtain," and their offense featured quarterback Terry Bradshaw and running back Franco Harris. After the 2005 season, Pittsburgh won the Super Bowl for the fifth time. Today, Pittsburgh fans wave "Terrible Towels" when they cheer on their team.

Baltimore is known for its strong defense. This defense is led by middle linebacker and Pro Bowler Ray Lewis. After the 2000 season, the Ravens beat the New York Giants 34-7 to win the Super Bowl.

After the 1995 season, the original Cleveland Browns team left Cleveland to become the Baltimore Ravens. A new Browns team started playing in 1999.

Cleveland has yet to win a Super Bowl, but before the Super Bowl was established, the Browns won four NFL championships. Top Browns players in the 1950s and 1960s include Hall of Famers Jim Brown and Otto Graham. Today, rowdy Cleveland fans sit in a section of the Browns' stadium called the "Dawg Pound." (Go back to page 44.) ◀◀

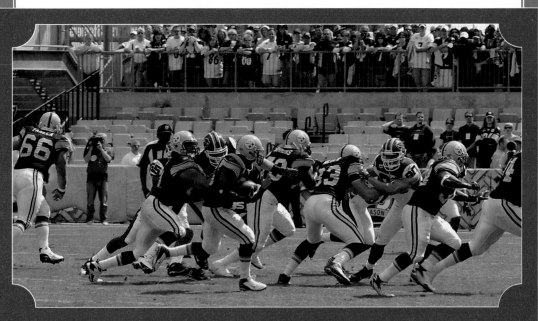

The Pittsburgh Steelers—one of Cincinnati's main rivals in the AFC North—are one of the National Football League's oldest franchises. This picture shows the team winning its 500th game in September 2007.

1978   Chad Johnson is born on January 9 in Los Angeles, California.

1995   Chad plays quarterback in his senior season at Miami Beach High School.

1996   Chad attends Langston University in Oklahoma, but he is kicked off the football team for fighting.

1997   Chad plays junior college football at Santa Monica College.

1998   Because of poor grades, Chad sits out a season of junior college football.

1999   Chad returns to Santa Monica to play for a second and final season.

2000   Chad enrolls at Oregon State University. He averages 21.8 yards per catch to help the Beavers earn a number four national ranking and win a Fiesta Bowl victory over Notre Dame.

2001   On April 21, the Cincinnati Bengals draft Chad with the fifth pick of the second round.

On September 30, Chad makes the first two catches of his NFL career in a game against the San Diego Chargers.

Chad finishes his rookie year with 329 receiving yards.

2002   Chad leads the Bengals in catches (69) and in receiving yardage (1,166).

2003   Chad's 1,355 receiving yards are the best in the AFC and set a Bengals single-season record.

Chad also catches ten touchdowns and is selected for the Pro Bowl.

2004   During the Pro Bowl, Chad grabs a 90-yard touchdown pass, the second-longest in the game's history.

Chad leads the AFC in receiving yards for a second straight year.

2005   Chad leads the AFC in receiving yards for a third straight season, setting a Bengals single-season record of 1,432 yards.

Chad also leads the AFC in catches, with 97 catches.

2006   In his first playoff appearance, Chad catches four passes for 59 yards in a loss to the Steelers.

Chad appears on the cover of the video game NFL Street 3.

Chad sets an NFL record for receiving yards in consecutive games, with a total of 450 yards in games against New Orleans and San Diego.

Becomes the first player in NFL history to lead a conference in receiving yards for four straight seasons.

2007   A crowd of 8,000 fans watch Chad defeat a horse in a race at River Downs.

On September 16 at Cleveland, Chad moves into the lead for all-time receiving yards for a Bengal, passing Isaac Curtis's record of 7,101 yards.

On November 25 against the Tennessee Titans, Chad records the 531st reception of his career, a Bengals record.

Chad returns to the Pro Bowl for a fifth straight year.

Career Statistics

Year	Team	Games	Rec	Yds	Avg	Lng	TD
2001	Bengals	12	28	329	11.8	28	1
2002	Bengals	16	69	1,166	16.9	72T	5
2003	Bengals	16	90	1,355	15.1	82T	10
2004	Bengals	16	95	1,274	13.4	53T	9
2005	Bengals	16	97	1,432	14.8	70T	9
2006	Bengals	16	87	1,369	15.7	74T	7
2007	Bengals	16	93	1,440	15.5	70T	8
TOTALS		108	559	8,365	15.0	82	49

Rec = receptions
Yds = yards
Avd = average yards per reception
Lng = longest reception (T indicates a touchdown)
TD = touchdown

Career Accomplishments

All-Pro selection, 2005, 2006
Pro Bowl selection, 2003, 2004, 2005, 2006, 2007
AFC leader in receiving yards, 2003, 2004, 2005, 2006
NFL leader in receiving yards, 2006

Cincinnati Bengals team records

Most receiving yards in a game (260)
Most receiving yards in a season (1,440)
Most touchdown receptions in a game (3, tied with several other players)
Most career receiving yards
Most career receptions

Books

Boyer, Mary Schmitt. *Welcome to the Jungle: Everything You Need to Know to Be a Bengals Fan*. Chicago: Triumph Books, 2008.

Daugherty, Paul. *Chad: I Can't Be Stopped*. Wilmington, OH: Orange Frazer Press, 2006

Gilbert, Sara. *The History of Cincinnati Bengals. NFL Today* series. Mankato, MN: Creative Education, 2004.

Mersch, Christine, and Jack Klumpe. *Cincinnati Bengals History*. Chicago: Arcadia Publishing, 2006.

Wheeler, Lonnie. *The Road Back: Cincinnati Bengals*. Wilmington, OH: Orange Frazer Press 2006.

Web Sites

www.chadjohnson85.com

The official Web site of Chad Johnson updates fans on news stories involving Chad and the Bengals. The site also features video of some of Chad's television commercials and a checklist that allows fans to vote on how Chad played in each game. Voting on the checklist helps raise money for Feed the Children.

www.cincinnatibengals.com

The official site of the Cincinnati Bengals offers in-depth coverage of the team.

www.nfl.com

The official Web site for the National Football League offers fans news about the league, its teams, and its players. This site has links to the Super Bowl, Pro Bowl, and Fantasy football leagues. During games, the site quickly offers in-game updates.

www.osubeavers.com

The official site of the Oregon State Beavers athletics offers fans video highlights, player profiles, and updated statistics for the various teams at Oregon State University.

www.feedthechildren.org

The official Web site for Feed the Children, a charitable organization Chad supports, offers information on how to help children in need around the world.

American Football Conference—one of the two conferences, or groups of teams, in the National Football League. The other group is called the National Football Conference (NFC). Both the AFC and NFC are further divided into four divisions, the North, South, East, and West Divisions.

cardiopulmonary resuscitation—a process that involves pushing on a person's chest and giving the person air through his or her mouth when the person has stopped breathing or his or her heart has stopped beating.

chicken dance—a group dance in which people imitate a chicken's motions, flapping their elbows like chicken wings, and then twisting their hips and clapping their hands.

contract—an agreement between two parties. In the NFL, these agreements are between players and teams and involve decisions on how many years the player will play for a specific team and how much the team will pay the player.

draft—the process by which NFL teams select new team members from among the nation's top college football players.

hold out—to resist or to wait for something you desire without giving in. In the NFL, a player can threaten to hold out and not participate in practices or games until the player's team agrees to give him a new contract.

interception—the stealing of a pass, usually thrown by the quarterback, by a member of the opposing team's defense.

ligament—a type of body tissue that holds one bone to another.

Monday Night Football—an NFL football game played on Monday night and broadcast on national television.

outpace—to move or run faster than someone or something else.

playoffs—a series of games played between the best football teams in a particular year to determine the players in that year's Super Bowl, a game that determines the NFL championship team.

recommend—to speak highly of or express confidence in someone or something.

scout—a person who works for a specific team and whose job it is to look for talented athletes to play for that team.

scout team—a group of back-up players who, during NFL team practices, work with and play against the starters on the NFL teams, helping the starters improve their play.

scouting combine—a series of practice drills and performance tests that athletes who want to play in the National Football League perform for NFL team scouts.

season ticket—a ticket that allows a fan to sit in the same seat for every home game in a season.

page 8 "He likes to be outspoken. . ." Karl Taro Greenfeld, "It's Good to Be Chad," *Sports Illustrated* (October 30, 2006), p. 58.

page 8 "How much of it. . ." Paul Daugherty, *Chad: I Can't Be Stopped* (Wilmington, OH: Orange Frazer Press, 2006), p. 164–165.

page 9 "I just want to tell. . ." Daugherty, *Chad: I Can't Be Stopped*, xv.

page 12 "He will never admit. . ." Greenfeld, "It's Good to Be Chad," p. 58

page 13 "If it weren't for football. . ." Lonnie Wheeler, "Surviving the Game," *Cincinnati Post* (October 2, 2003).

page 14 "He was almost. . ." *ESPN* Interview, available at Youtube.com. http://www.youtube.com/watch?v= IMIXwc9VPsc&feature=related

page 17 "I'm looking to do . . ." Mel Kiper, "Q&A with Chad Johnson," ESPN.com (February 20, 2001). http://espn.go.com/ melkiper/s/2001/0215/1085985.html

page 18 "We looked at each other. . ." *ESPN* Interview.

page 19 "I said this was. . ." Daugherty, *Chad: I Can't Be Stopped,* xiv.

page 19 "We're like family . . ." Greenfeld, "It's Good to be Chad," p. 58.

page 21 "You have the opportunity. . ." Daugherty, *Chad: I Can't Be Stopped*, p. 100.

page 22 "I didn't have anyone. . ." Daugherty, *Chad: I Can't Be Stopped*, p. 98.

page 22 "I told him, . . ." Jason Williams, "After a Breakout Season, Wide Receiver Chad Johnson Now Wants to 'Dominate the Game'," *Cincinnati Post* (September 6, 2003), p. D1.

page 24 "That's having my back . . . " ESPN.go.com (November 16, 2003). http://sports.espn.go.com/nfl/recap? gameId=231116004.

page 25 "That's the whole point. . . ." Dennis Dillon, "Overnight Success," *The Sporting News*, (October 4, 2004), p. 26.

page 27 "This game was. . . ." Kevin Allen, "Bengals Win Lopsided Catfight vs. Lions, Claim AFC North Title," *USA Today* (December 19, 2005). http://www.usatoday.com/sports/ football/games/2005-12-18-bengals-lions_x.htm.

page 29 "When a guy gets open . . . " "Bengals Jump All Over Vikings 37-8," NFL.com (July 26, 2007). http://www.nfl.com/gamecenter/recap? displayPage=tab_recap&game_id=285 43&season=2005&week=REG2.

page 30 "Usually, what makes. . ." Tony Bruno, "My Turn," *The Sporting News* (April 14, 2006).

page 30 "My name isn't Chad. . ." Cincinnati Bengals press conference, 2006, available on Youtube. http://www.youtube. com/watch?v=ifeJ_3NA6IU

page 31 "I don't know why . . ." Michael Silver, interview with Chad Johnson, *Sports Illustrated* 105, no. 15 (October 16, 2006), p. 29.

page 32 "He thinks he can. . ." Daugherty, *Chad: I Can't Be Stopped*, p. 7.

page 33 "All I do is make. . ." Bruno, "My Turn."

page 35 "There are a lot of . . ." "Tomlinson Scores Four TDs as Chargers Turn Back Bengals," ESPN.go.com (November 12, 2006). http://sports.espn.go.com/nfl/recap?gameId=261112004.

page 35 "I'm trying to. . ." "Palmer Leads Bengals in Win over Saints," NFL.com (November 19, 2006). http://www.nfl.com/gamecenter/recap;jsessionid=1FA0F022DF27D11D6CFBDD78FC9ADCB2?game_id=29013&displayPage=tab_recap&season=2006&week=REG11

page 38 "He's quick. . . ." Dustin Dow, "Chad Johnson Beats Horse in Race," *Cincinnati Enquirer/USA Today* (May 31, 2007). http://www.usatoday.com/sports/football/nfl/bengals/2007-06-09-johnson-horse_N.htm

page 39 "It's all for fun . . ." Quoted in "Chad Johnson Will Race Horse for Charity," *USA Today* (June 2, 2007). http://www.usatoday.com/sports/football/nfl/bengals/2007-06-02-johnson-horse_N.htm

page 40 "My checklist has always. . ." Business Wire press release, "Football Star Chad Johnson Asks America," (September 15, 2006).

page 41 "This is a big honor. . ." Wireless News press release, "EA Taps Cincinnati Bengals' . . . " (August 25, 2006).

page 41 "He's a live-for-the-moment. . ." Daugherty, *Chad: I Can't Be Stopped*, p. 125.

page 42 "My job keeps me. . ." Greenfeld, "It's Good to Be Chad," p. 58.

page 42 "Chad has broken down. . ." Daugherty, *Chad: I Can't Be Stopped*, p. 138.

page 45 "We've made it clear. . ." Peter King, "Monday Morning Quarterback," *Sports Illustrated* (May 6, 2008). http://sportsillustrated.cnn.com/2008/writers/peter_king/05/06/mailbag/index.html

page 45 "I think he could . . . " Dennis Dillon, "Overnight Success," p. 26.

Allen, Jason, 4, **7**
American Football Conference (AFC), 6, 25, 53
    division title, 26–27, 30
Anderson, Ken, 52

Belichick, Bill, 50
Bly, Dre, 26
Bodden, Leigh, 29
Bradshaw, Terry, 53
Bratkowski, Bob, 18–19, 22
Brown, Eddie, 34
Brown, Jim, 53
Brown, Mike, 50
Brown, Paul, 46, 47, 51
Bryant, Kobe, 39

Carson Palmer Foundation, 52
charity work, 38–41
Cincinnati, Ohio, 46, 49, 50
Cincinnati Bengals, 9
    2002 season, 21–22
    2003 season, 22–25
    2004 season, 25
    2005 season, 26–33
    2006 season, 33–35
    2007 season, 4–5, **7**, 36–38, 42–45
    draft Johnson, 18–20
    and Johnson's rookie year, 20–21
    and the playoffs, 27, 30–33
    and the Super Bowl, 51
    uniforms, 47
    See also Johnson, Chad
Collins, Charles, 14, 18
Cooksey, Patti, 38
Curtis, Isaac, 44

draft, NFL, 16–20

Erickson, Dennis, 14, 18–19
Esiason, Boomer, 51

Feed the Children, 39–40
Flowers, Bessie Mae (grandmother), 12–13, 16
Flowers, James (grandfather), 10, 12–13

Gardner, Rod, 16
Gordon, Jeff, 39
Graham, Otto, 53

Harris, Franco, 53
Heisman Trophy, 25, 52
Henry, Chris, 31
Houshmandzadeh, T.J., 6, 19–20, 38, **43**, 48

Jackson, Hue, 32
James, LeBron, 39
Johnson, Billy ("White Shoes"), 51
Johnson, Butch, 51
Johnson, Chad, 9
    birth and childhood, 10–13
    and charity work, 38–41
    and earnings, 45
    and endorsements, 40, 41
    and fines, 6, 30
    and grades, 13–14
    in high school, 13
    and injuries, 21, 35
    and legal troubles, 14
    mother and siblings of, 12–13, 14
    and the NFL draft, 16–20

and "Ocho Cinco" nickname, 6, 30, **31**
at Oregon State University, 14–15, 48
and parenthood, 41–42
and the playoffs, 27, 30–33
and the Pro Bowl, 6, 20, **24**, 25, **43**
records of, 5, 25, 33–34, 35, 42, 44
and the Restore the Roar race, 38–39
rookie year, 20–21
at Santa Monica Junior College, 14, 48
statistics, 6, **20**, **24**, 25, **37**, 42
and touchdown celebrations, 6, 8, 29–30, **31**, 33, 38, 51
    See also Cincinnati Bengals
Johnson, Keyshawn, 13
Johnson, Rudi, 23

Kiper, Mel, **17**
Kitna, Jon, 21–22, 25, 31

Lewis, Marvin, 22, 32, 33, 41, 42, 45, 50
Lewis, Ray, 53
Liberty City, Miami, 5, 12

Marvin Lewis Community Fund, 50
Mayweather, Floyd, 39
Miami Beach High School, 13
Mitchell, Freddie, 16
Montana, Joe, 51

Numbers in **bold italics** refer to captions.

Morgan, Quincy, 18
Moss, Randy, 6, 42
Moss, Santana, 16

National Football League
  (NFL)
    divisions, 53
    draft, 16–20
    fines Johnson, 6, 30
NFL Street 3 game, *40*, 41

"Ocho Cinco," 6, 30, *31*
  See also Johnson, Chad
Ohio River, 49
Oregon State University,
  14–15, 48

Palmer, Carson, 4, 25, 29,
  31, 33, *34*, 38, 52
Paul Brown Stadium, 46
Pro Bowl, 6, 20, *24*, 25, *43*,
  48

Restore the Roar race,
  38–39
Robinson, Koren, 16
Rolle, Samari, 13

Sanders, Deion, 22, 45
Santa Monica Junior College,
  14
Schulters, Lance, 4
Sims, Dale, 13

Smith, Steve, 6, 8, 14, 30–31, 48
Super Bowl, 9, 33, 51

Terrell, David, 16
Tomlinson, LaDainian, 34

Von Oelhoffen, Kimo, 31

Warrick, Peter, 18, 20, 23
Wayne, Reggie, 16
Welker, Wes, 48
Woods, Ickey, 51
Wright, Elmo, 51
Wyche, Sam, 51

Yarber, Eric, 48

Frank Angst lives in Lexington, Kentucky, where he covers horse racing for the *Thoroughbred Times*. He graduated from Butler University in 1990 and has covered sports for nearly 20 years. Angst covered the Cincinnati Bengals while working for the *Portsmouth Daily Times*, and he covered Marshall University football and basketball while writing for the *Charleston Gazette*. Angst has worked for the *Thoroughbred Times* for the past six years, where he was honored with first place and third place awards from the American Horse Publications for stories written in 2005 and 2006.

PICTURE CREDITS

page

5: Amy Sia/SPCS

7: Jeffrey M. Boan/El Nuevo Herald/MCT

8: Greg Rust/Bengals/SPCS

11: Mark Ashman/Walt Disney World/PRMS

12: T&T/IOA Photo

15: cornfusion/SPCS

17: George Bridges/KRT

19: Greg Rust/Bengals/SPCS

20: Cincinnati Enquirer/KRT

23: Cincinnati Enquirer/KRT

24: Kirby Lee/NFL/WireImage

27: Eric Eckel/SPCS

28: G.N. Lawrence/WireImage

31: Dan Beineke/NFL/WireImage

32: kemosabee/SPCS

34: Cincinnati Enquirer/KRT

37: Rob Moyer/AASI Photos

39: Max & Murphy/AASI Photos

40: EA Sports/NMI

43: IOS Photos

44: T&T/IOA Photos

46: Derek Jenson/T&T/IOA Photos

47: Greg Rust/Bengals/SPCS

49: Ohio Div. of Travel & Tourism/PRMS

50: Greg Rust/Bengals/SPCS

52: Greg Rust/Bengals/SPCS

53: Michael Rooney/SPCS

Front cover: Jeff Gross/Getty Images
Front cover inset: Mike Zarrilli/Getty Images